Bollynatyam®

Dancing India!

Created by Sangita Shresthova

Illustrated by Iva Fafková

Bollynatyam®

WELCOME!

Welcome to *Dancing India!*, a coloring book inspired by India's jubilant, intricate, and lively dances. The collection features thirty pictures inspired by Indian classical dances, folk traditions, and a touch of Bollywood. We invite you to bring a little fun into your life as you experience the rich world of Indian dance. Let the coloring begin!

Founded by Sangita Shresthova, Bollynatyam® takes a historically and culturally sensitive approach to contemporary Indian and South Asian dance. Our teaching and choreography draws on classical Indian dance (Bharatanatyam), martial arts, contemporary movement, and Bollywood dance.

For more information see: *www.bollynatyam.com*

Dancing India!: Coloring Book

Ancient Indian temple carvings come to life as this dancer strikes a time-honored pose from Bharatanatyam, a South Indian dance tradition.

Balancing three pots on her head is not enough of a challenge, this folk dancer stands on them too.

An ornamental belt accentuates this dancer's hip movements.

Do card games and dance go together? Everything is possible in this Bollywood song-and-dance sequence.

This dancer leaps into the air, celebrating the music she hears.

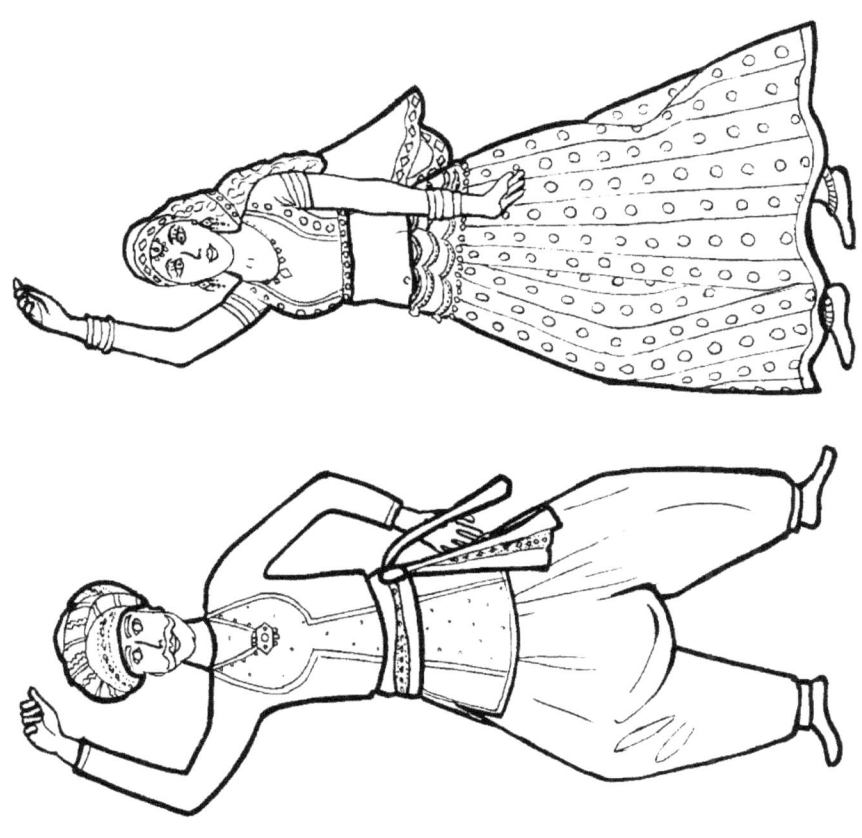

Moving in unison, this dancing pair shares a special moment.

Dancers need hours to prepare for a Kathakali (South Indian dance) performance. Every part of the face, even the eyebrows and nostrils, become part of the dance.

Sword in mouth, pots balanced on head, and hand cymbals are all part of this Rajasthani folk dance.

Background dancers wave their flags as they celebrate India's Independence Day.

Elaborate embroidery and glittery mirror-work accentuate this Indian dance performance.

The dancers twirl with joy as they celebrate Diwali, India's festival of lights.

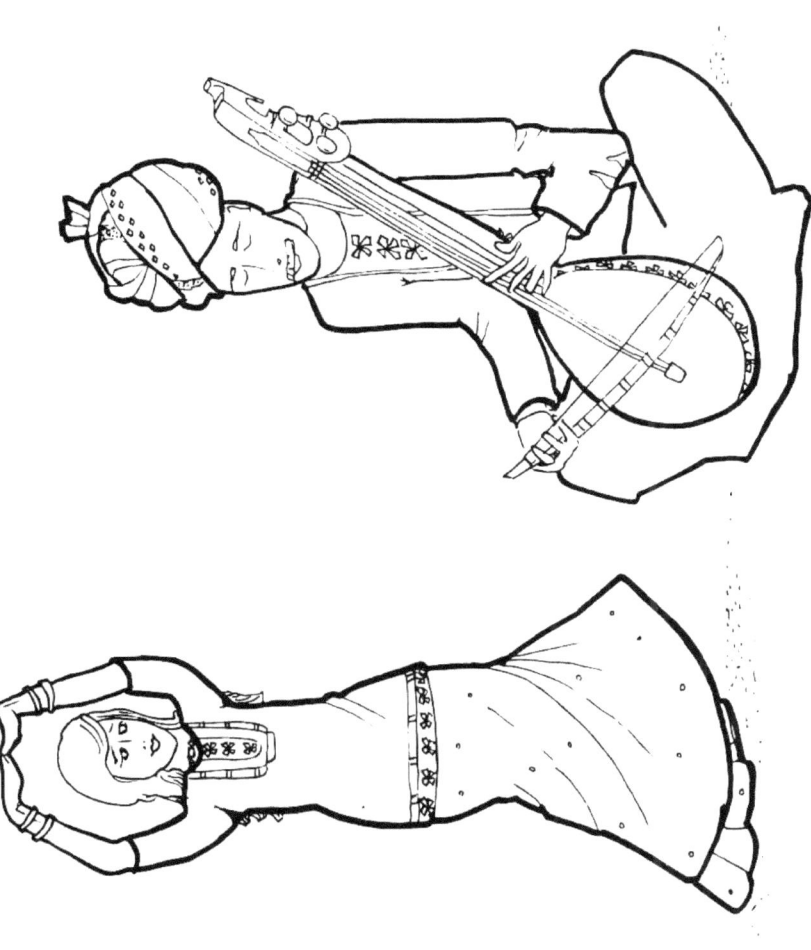

The sweet melodies created by the sarangi entice the dancer to join in.

Bollywood dancers adapt Indian classical dance gestures to share stories and emotions.

Arms spread, and feet in movement! This dancer asks
everyone to join her in her joyous dance.

Elephants are part of India's traditions.

"Come and dance with me!" A dancer invites the luminous full moon to join her.

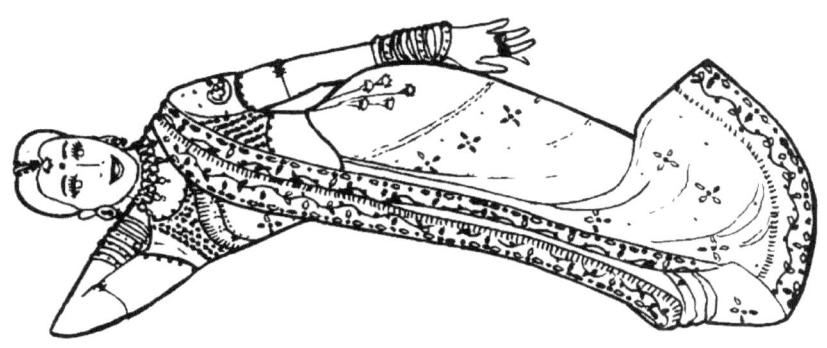

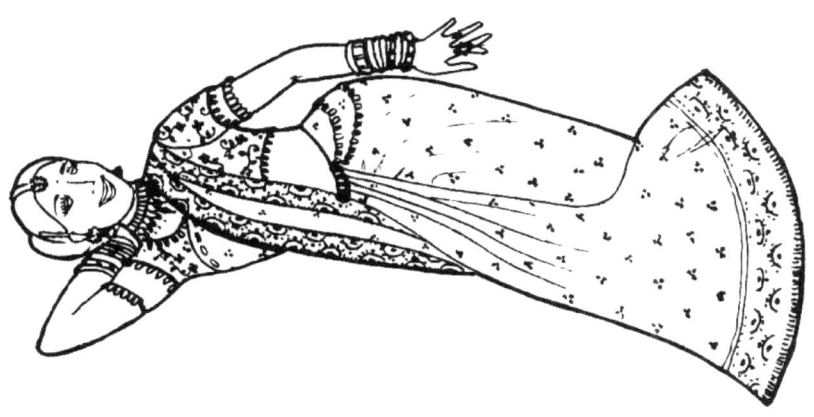

Their hearts swayed with their hips. All these dancers needed for their duet was an Indian dance beat.

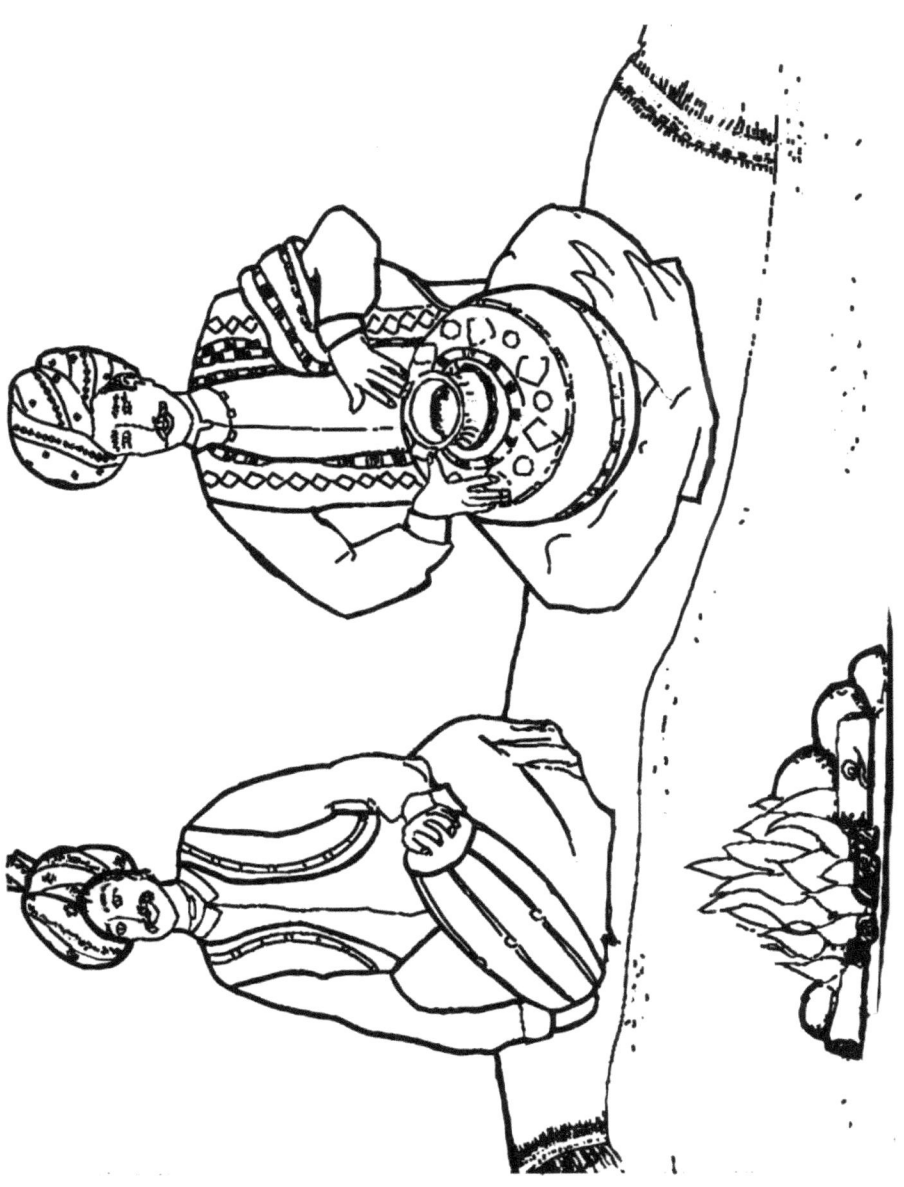

Rhythm or *tala* is a key element of Indian dance.

The dancer swings her arms with pure joy in this Rajasthani folk dance.

Dance happens everywhere in Indian films, even on the roof of a moving train.

Whirl! Whirl! And, whirl once more! Fast turns and percussive footwork define Kathak, a north Indian dance tradition.

Odissi is a dance tradition from the state of Orissa, located on India's eastern coast.

The festivities are off to a great start as the dancers perform their spontaneous duet.

This dancer lifts her skirt to accentuate the elaborate footwork characteristic of Indian dance.

A costumed horse becomes part of the dance in this Indian folk performance.

Earthen pots are practical for carrying and cooling water. They are also a useful dance prop.

This dancer accompanies himself on the Ektara, a traditional Indian stringed instrument.

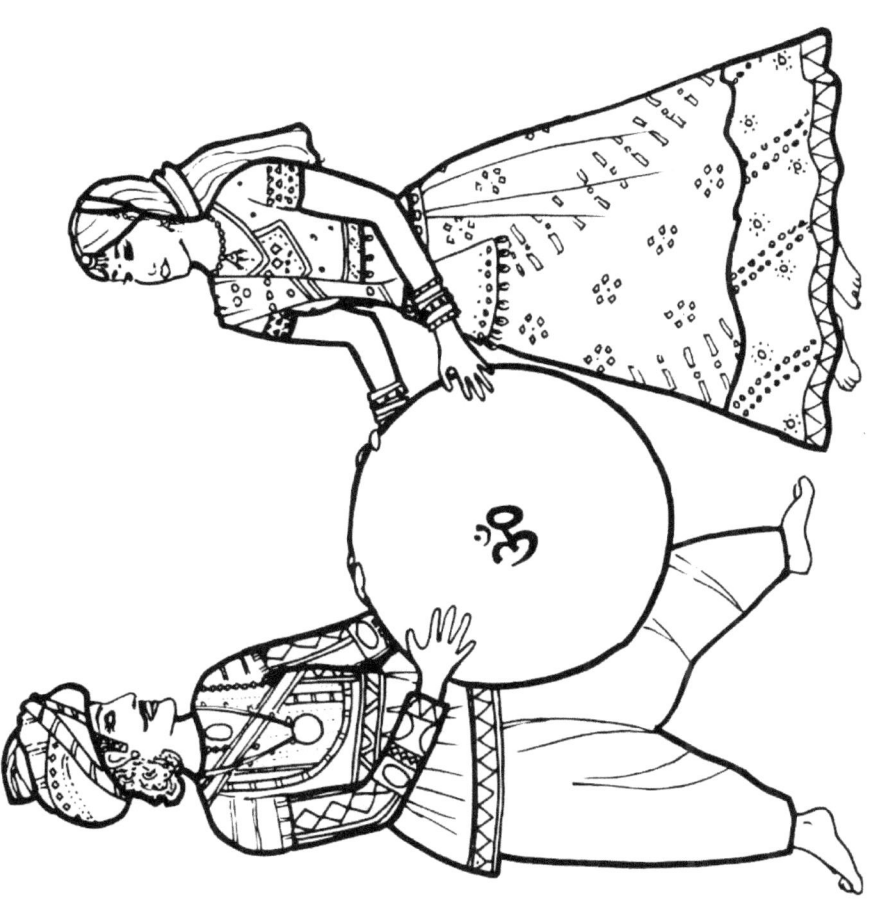

The large drum is decorated with an 'Om', which symbolizes the eternal triad of existence in Hinduism.

Ta-ka-dhee-mee-ta-kee-ta. Stamping complex rhythmic patterns requires skill and practice.

Dancing at weddings is a true Indian pastime.

www.ingramcontent.com/pod-product-compliance
Lightning Source LLC
Chambersburg PA
CBHW071120280526
45787CB00003B/1117